Collective Biographies

AMERICAN WOMEN OF FLIGHT

Pilots and Pioneers

Henry M. Holden

Enslow Publishers, Inc.

40 Industrial Road	PO Box 38
Box 398	Aldershot
Berkeley Heights, NJ 07922	Hants GU12 6BP
USA	UK

http://www.enslow.com

My thanks to all within these pages who contributed their time to read their biographies and supplied personal photos.

Library of Congress Cataloging-in-Publication Data

Holden, Henry M.
    American women of flight : pilots and pioneers / by Henry M. Holden.
       p. cm.—(Collective biographies)
    Includes bibliographical references and index.
    Summary: Ten biographies of women aviators, including Harriet Quimby, Bessie Coleman, Amelia Earhart, Anne Morrow Lindbergh, Jacqueline Cochran, Betty Skelton Frankman, Bonnie Tiburzi, Nelda Lee, Colonel Eileen Collins, and Martha King.
    ISBN 0-7660-2005-3
    1. Women air pilots—Biography—Juvenile literature. [1. Air pilots.
    2. Women—Biography.] I. Title.
II. Series.
    TL539.H563 2002
    629.13'092'273—dc21

                     2001006702

Printed in the United States of America

10 9 8 7 6 5 4 3 2 1

To Our Readers:
We have done our best to make sure all Internet Addresses in this book were active and appropriate when we went to press. However, the author and the publisher have no control over and assume no liability for the material available on those Internet sites or on other Web sites they may link to. Any comments or suggestions can be sent by e-mail to comments@enslow.com or to the address on the back cover.

Every effort has been made to locate all copyright holders of material used in this book. If any errors or omissions have occurred, corrections will be made in future editions of this book.

Illustration Credits: Aviation Hall of Fame, Pat Reilly, pp. 26, 38, 43, 46, 52; Eileen Collins, p. 84; Betty Skelton Frankman, pp. 56, 61; Martha King, pp. 94, 99; Library of Congress, pp. 11, 31; National Aeronautics and Space Administration, p. 90; National Air and Space Museum, Smithsonian Institution, pp. 6, 16, 21; Bonnie Tiburzi, pp. 66, 72; Nelda Lee, pp. 76, 81.

Cover Illustrations: Eileen Collins, bottom left; Aviation Hall of Fame, Pat Reilly, top left; National Air and Space Museum, Smithsonian Institution, top right; Bonnie Tiburzi, bottom right.

Contents

Preface

Today women's roles in aviation vary from airline pilots to astronauts. However, in earlier times, women were discouraged from participating in the risky pursuits of flight. Nevertheless, women aviators proved they were as capable of piloting planes as men. Throughout aviation history, women were at the forefront flying undeveloped aircraft through uncharted territories. Most faced prejudice and discrimination, but they refused to give up.

"Flying is not one for which women are physically qualified. They lack strength and presence of mind and the courage to excel as aviators. It is a man's sport and pastime."[1] This was the general frame of mind toward women during early aviation. While there were no laws prohibiting women from being pilots, everyday society reflected these biases. Although women pioneers proved they could fly, and in many cases broke records held by men, they were still not given equal treatment. In spite of that, women continued to make strides toward pursuing careers in aviation.

In fact, women pilots have been flying airplanes for more than ninety years, and the participation of women in aviation dates back to the earliest flights. Early flying was much more dangerous than it is today because it was still in the development stage. Accidents were quite common.

The first American woman to fly was Lucretia Bradley, in a gas-filled balloon. She flew from Easton, Pennsylvania, to Phillipsburg, New Jersey, in 1855.[2] Although fewer than half-a-dozen of these types of flights were documented, many first flights made by women were in lighter-than-air crafts such as hot air balloons.

The ten stories of women aviators highlighted in this book show women who had the courage to stand up to the prejudices and biases of others and to the challenge of flight. Their lives are inspirational and encouraging. Although they chose different paths in their pursuit to fly, each of their stories has one clear message in common—you are limited only by your dreams and your enthusiasm to make them happen.

Harriet Quimby

Harriet Quimby
(1875 –1912)

On April 16, 1912, Harriet Quimby sat in her airplane at the airfield in Dover, England. At 5:30 A.M., she took off and pointed the airplane toward the coast of France, about twenty-two miles across the English Channel. The English Channel is the body of water between England and France. "In a moment I was in the air, climbing steadily in a long circle. I was up to 1,500 feet in thirty seconds. From this high point of vantage my eyes lit at once on Dover Castle. It was half hidden in a fog bank. I felt that trouble was coming . . . "[1]

Harriet Quimby was born on May 11, 1875, on a farm near Coldwater, Michigan. She was the younger of two daughters born to William and Ursula (Cook) Quimby.[2]

Harriet was about nine years old when her family moved to Arroyo Grande, California. Her father tried to provide for his family by farming. Little is known about Harriet's teen years.

By 1901, Quimby was living in San Francisco. At a time when most women were expected to stay at home and raise families, Quimby worked as a journalist. She wrote articles about issues such as child labor and the environment. Some of her early writings appeared in the *Sunday Call* newspaper.[3]

In 1902, Quimby moved to New York City, where there were more opportunities for writers. While in New York, she wrote the first of more than 350 articles that appeared in the pages of *Leslie's Illustrated Weekly* newspaper.

By 1906, Quimby was one of *Leslie's Illustrated Weekly's* travel writers. She learned to use a camera and became a photojournalist. Many of her travel articles about Cuba, the Middle East, and Europe were illustrated with her photographs.

In 1910, Quimby saw her first monoplane. "The very first time I saw a monoplane was at the last day of the aviation meet at Hempstead. . . . I saw one of the aviators make an exhibition flight, and I thought to myself, 'Really, it looks quite easy; I believe I could do it myself'—and, after a minute I resolved, 'And I will.'"[4]

However, there were not many flying schools that would accept women. "Men did not want us driving motorcars, much less airplanes," said Matilde Moisant, Quimby's close friend. Moisant, however, had a good connection—her brother Alfred owned a flying school. In the spring of 1911, Matilde Moisant and Harriet Quimby began flying lessons at the Moisant Flying School on Long Island.

Quimby arrived at the field at 4:00 A.M. to take lessons. After several lessons, she felt she was ready to earn her pilot's license. On the day of testing, she climbed into a Moisant monoplane, dressed in a jacket and trousers of wool-backed satin, with leather puttees (leg wraps), heavy goggles, and a big aviation cap.

Quimby had planned to keep her flying lessons a secret from the public. She did not want the fact that she was a woman to interfere with her lessons. She wore a large hat and goggles as a disguise. After the wind blew a covering away from her face during a walk to a lesson, her identity was revealed.[5]

News that a woman was trying to earn her pilot's license spread quickly. Newspaper headlines shouted, "Woman in Trousers, A Daring Air Pilot." Curious spectators gathered at the field.

To earn her pilot's license, Quimby had to complete three tasks. First, her plane had to reach an altitude of 164 feet. Second, she had to fly five right and left turns, known as "figure eights" around pylons (tall poles). And third, she was required to land within 100 feet from where the plane had left the ground.[6]

The crowd watched as Quimby successfully completed the first and second part of the test by reaching an altitude of 164 feet and doing a series of spiral curves, making a figure eight in the air. On the final part of the test, Quimby set a world's record when she landed within seven feet, four inches of the given mark.

After the flight, Quimby confidently climbed out of her airplane with oil from the engine covering her face and walked over to the officials and asked, "Well, do I get that license?"

"We guess you do," the officials replied.[7]

On August 1, 1911, Quimby became the first American woman to earn her pilot's license. Quimby was the second woman in the world to earn her license. The first was Raymonde de la Roche of France, in 1910.

"I took up flying," Quimby told reporters, "because I thought I'd like the sensation, and I have not regretted it. I like driving, but after seeing airplanes, I couldn't resist the challenge."

"Once I had my license," said Quimby, "I realized I could share the thrills of aviation with my readers." In *Leslie's Illustrated Weekly*, she called her adventures, "How a Woman Learns To Fly," and "The Dangers of Flying and How to Avoid Them."

Quimby also realized that the flying outfit she had worn for her lessons and the exam were not very feminine. "The very first thing the women who resolves to be a flyer must do is to abandon skirts and don (put on) a knickerbockers uniform for the reasons that are self-evident."[8] Quimby believed skirts were dangerous for women who fly because

Harriet Quimby was the first woman to pilot an airplane across the English Channel.

they could fly up and block the vision of the pilot while flying.

Quimby had an aviation suit made for her by a tailor. She said it was to "establish proper dress" for women pilots, who may have been apprehensive about looking too masculine in pants. Pants were seen as improper dress for women at that time.

The flying suit consisted of a tailor-made, hooded, one-piece, purple, thick wool and satin outfit with knee length pants and high-laced black leather boots. With the outfit, she wore flying goggles and elbow-length gloves. The suit could also be converted into a walking skirt, a type of skirt common for that period.

Quimby began flying at air meets. On September 4, 1911, at Staten Island, New York, a crowd of twenty-thousand people watched, as she became the first woman to fly at night.

Quimby also wanted to be the first woman to pilot an airplane across the English Channel. She told her plan to Gustave Hamel, an aviator friend. He doubted that Quimby had the ability to pilot an airplane across the Channel. He suggested Quimby dress in her flying gear and go to a destination spot, while he fly across the Channel in her place and land in a remote spot. Then Quimby could take the credit for the trip.

"The extraordinary offer . . . amused me most of all," said Quimby. "I laughed and told him I was going to make the flight myself." Quimby did not accept his offer but requested he teach her to read a compass.[9]

During the flight, Quimby's plane went off course. Hamel warned that if she drifted off course by as little as five miles over the North Sea, she could get lost and probably go down in the icy waters.

Hamel gave Quimby only a brief training in reading a compass. "I had never before used a compass, and I was somewhat doubtful of my ability to do so."[10]

Quimby followed the compass needle faithfully as she flew though the dense fog. Soon, a gleaming strip of white sand caught her eye. She landed at a beach near Hardelot, France.

Her victory did not get much recognition. The trip was drowned out by news reports on the sinking of the *Titanic*, a large ocean liner that was thought to be unsinkable.

However, on April 18, 1912, an editorial in *The New York Times* commented on Quimby's trip, ". . . a thing done first is one thing: done for the seventh or eighth time it is quite different, of course it still proves ability and capacity, but it doesn't prove equality."

Quimby had said shortly after earning her license, "I did not want to be the first American woman to fly just for the publicity," said Quimby. "I just want to be first . . . I have written so much about other people . . . I enjoy sitting back and reading about myself for once. I think that's excusable in me."[11]

On July 1, 1912, Quimby attended the Boston Air Meet. She took off toward the Boston lighthouse with the manager of the event as a passenger. She was at 5,000 feet and coming out of a turn around the lighthouse. Suddenly, the plane flipped nose down. The shocked crowd watched, helplessly. First, her passenger, and then Quimby fell from the plane. Both were killed.

Before her death, Quimby wrote an article for *Good Housekeeping* magazine. In it, she gave her opinion on aviation as a career for women. The article appeared September 1912, two months after her fatal crash. "I think," she said, "the aeroplane should open a fruitful occupation for women. I see no reason they cannot realize handsome incomes by carrying passengers between adjacent towns, from parcel delivery, taking photographs or conducting schools of flying."

Harriet Quimby's vision has come true. Today there are women airline pilots, military pilots, and private pilots. On April 27, 1991, the U.S. Postal Service issued a 50-cent airmail stamp in Quimby's honor.

2

Bessie Coleman
(1892–1926)

No one had ever heard of a black woman pilot in 1918. There were a few women pilots of course, but a black woman pilot? Bessie Coleman changed all that. At a time when lynching and segregation were prevalent in the African-American community, Coleman was determined to fly.

After she was denied access to flight training schools in the United States, she learned to speak French and traveled to France to complete her lessons. She returned to the United States on June 15, 1921, as the first black—man or woman—in the world to earn a pilot's license.

Elizabeth (Bessie) Coleman was born in Atlanta, Texas, on January 26, 1892. She was the tenth of thirteen children born to Susan and George

Bessie Coleman

Coleman. Four of the children died. Bessie's parents were sharecroppers. George Coleman was African American and part Cherokee,[1] Susan Coleman was African American.

When Bessie was very young, her family moved to Waxahachie, Texas and worked as tenant farmers. As tenant farmers they farmed land owned by someone else and paid rent in money or crops to the owner. Bessie's early life was filled with dirt roads, tenant farms, and endless labor.

When Bessie was seven years old, her father wanted his family to go with him to the Indian Territory in Oklahoma. Indian Territories were regions set aside to make homes for Indians from about 1830 to 1906. The Indians had been moved from their original homes after white settlers wanted to take over the lands on which the Indians had lived.

Susan Coleman refused to go. George Coleman returned to the territory without his family, and Susan Coleman raised her children alone.

From an early age, Bessie's mother urged all of her children to get an education. Susan Coleman could not read herself; however, she knew education was important. In the evenings, Bessie's older brother would read stories from the Bible. And Susan Coleman made it a point to borrow books from a book wagon that visited the neighborhood once or twice a year. She wanted all her children to learn through reading.

Susan Coleman also insisted that her children attend school. At six years old, Bessie walked four miles to a one-room schoolhouse that often had no paper or pencils. When Bessie learned to read, she found a brand-new world in books. She said she loved reading more than playing with dolls.

During this time, schools were segregated. Black and white children could not attend the same school. In fact, many things were separated by color—"white only" or "colored only." These were called Jim Crow laws. These laws did not permit African Americans to live, attend school, or visit public places without unfair restrictions. Despite the lack of many things and the long trip to get to school, Bessie managed to finish the required eight grades of school. This was a great accomplishment because graduating from high school was unusual for African-American women during that time.

Susan Coleman encouraged Bessie to attend college. Unfortunately, her mother could not afford to send her. Bessie took in laundry and ironing to save up the tuition money, and then she enrolled in Colored Agricultural and Normal University in Langston, Oklahoma. She ran out of money after one term and went back to Texas to work in a laundry. Feeling unhappy, she decided to make a change.

At the age of twenty-three, Coleman moved to Chicago to join her two older brothers. There she enrolled in Burnham School of Beauty and Culture. After she finished, she found work as a manicurist. She worked for William Buckner, a Chicago White Sox trainer and the owner of the White Sox Barbershop.

During this time, Bessie's brother Walter Coleman introduced Bessie to Claude Glenn, who was fourteen years older than her. They were secretly married on January 30, 1917. No one was aware of the marriage and the two never lived together. Information that the two were married was not found until years later.[2]

Coleman's interest in aviation began when she heard stories of wild flying adventures from soldiers returning from World War I. Newspapers across the country reported on the adventures. Coleman became convinced she should also be flying and not just reading and hearing about it.

She began searching libraries for information on flying and training schools. She planned to attend a training school to learn to fly. However, Coleman found that two strikes were held against her. First, she was a woman. And second, she was African American. She found there were a few flying schools that would teach a woman; however, there were none that would teach an African-American woman.

Coleman visited the office of Robert S. Abbott. He was the founder and editor of the *Chicago Defender*, a major African-American newspaper. She asked for his help to get her enrolled in flying school. Abbott, a prominent citizen of Chicago, was excited by the idea but knew it would be difficult to find a school that would accept African Americans. He suggested that Coleman take flying lessons in France. France was more accepting toward people of color.

Coleman took Abbott's advice and went to school. She attended a Berlitz school in Chicago,[3] a school known for teaching people to speak other languages. For additional income, she helped operate a chili parlor. In a few months, she had learned enough French for her trip. She used her savings from her work as a manicurist and manager of the chili parlor, coupled with financial support from Abbott, to finance her trip to Europe.

Coleman left the United States in November 1920, and by June 15, 1921, Coleman had earned her pilot's license. She had made her dream come true. Like most French pilots, she learned to fly in a *Nieuport*, a 27-foot single-engine biplane. A biplane is an airplane with two wings, one above the other. She became the only African-American licensed pilot in the world.

Coleman returned to the United States in 1921 with both African-American and white reporters waiting to meet her. Many were excited to see the first African-American licensed pilot. During a stop in New York City, she was invited as a guest of honor to attend the first all-black Broadway musical *Shuffle Along*. During the musical, she received a standing ovation from the African-American and white audience members. The cast gave her a silver cup with the names of the cast members engraved on it.[4]

"The sky is the only place where there is no prejudice. Up there everyone is equal. Everyone is free." Bessie Coleman encouraged African Americans to learn to fly.

Soon after her homecoming, Coleman found she could not find a pilot's job. She dreamed of putting on fantastic flying shows filled with aerial tricks and stunts. However, the show required flying skills that she did not have. Again, Coleman left for Europe. This time she went to Germany for advanced training. Her goal was to qualify as a stunt pilot. She completed her mission.

Coleman returned to the United States in August 1923. It was time to begin her new flying career. In her first appearance in an air show the following month, she dressed in a military-style uniform. There were no women military pilots during World War I so this promoted an exciting image. She knew the publicity would attract paying audiences. Robert Abbott and the *Chicago Defender* sponsored the event and promoted her as "Bessie World's Greatest Woman Flyer." By October of 1922 when she appeared in an air show in Chicago, she owned three Curtiss JN-4 "Jenny" airplanes.[5]

Her next goal was to open a flying school and teach other African-American men and women to fly. She raised the funds she needed for the school by giving flying exhibitions and lecturing on aviation. The curiosity of seeing an African-American woman drew large crowds wherever she went. Crowds of spectators who initially came because they were curious discovered Coleman could fly and were impressed by her skill. Once they saw her talents, they knew why she was called "Queen Bess" by the *Chicago Defender*.

Like many of the early stunt pilots, Coleman had several flying accidents. Her first occurred in February 1923 in Santa Monica, California. She was at 300 feet when the engine in her plane failed. The airplane fell to the ground and was completely destroyed.

The accident did not stop her. Although she suffered a broken leg and several broken ribs in the crash, she would not quit. When her broken bones healed, she went right back to performing at air shows.

Coleman made it a point to refuse to perform unless African Americans could be permitted to see her. Once, Coleman was invited to give an exhibition in Waxahachie, Texas. When Coleman arrived, the officials said that African Americans would not be allowed in to see her show. She refused to fly until the officials agreed to let African Americans into the show. They agreed to her demands.

Her demands raised more than a few eyebrows and some believed her demands would put her in danger. Also the Jenny plane she planned to fly was dangerous. The engines were notorious for failing in flight. However, nothing would stop her, not even the warnings from her friends and family who feared for her safety.

On April 30, 1926, she almost had enough money saved to open her own flying school. She had been attracting national attention. Coleman was scheduled to fly the next day in a May 1 celebration in Orlando, Florida. That evening, Coleman took her plane up for a test flight. With her was mechanic and promoter, William Wills. Wills had flown the plane to deliver it to Coleman a few days earlier. He had made two emergency landings on the flight over because of engine trouble.

According to eyewitnesses, Coleman and Wills had been in the air for about twelve minutes. They were at an altitude of about 3,000 feet. Suddenly, the airplane tipped nose down and went into a 110-mile per hour power dive and flipped over.[6] Coleman's seatbelt was not fastened and she did not have on a parachute. Coleman was thrown from the plane and plunged to her death. Wills tried to straighten the plane, but when he could not, it crashed. Wills was trapped in the plane.

Minutes after the crash, a bystander nervously lit a cigarette. The spark ignited the spilled gasoline from the plane. The wreckage with Wills's body trapped inside went up in flames. A later investigation found a loose wrench had jammed the controls.

Coleman's friends returned her body to Chicago, the city she loved. On the tenth anniversary of her death, Abbott wrote an editorial in the *Chicago Defender*. "Though with the crashing of the plane life ceased for Bessie Coleman, she inspired enough members of her race by her courage to carry on in aviation. What they accomplish will stand as a memorial to Miss Coleman."[7] Today, more than seventy-five years after her death, she is still inspiring young African-American women.

On April 27, 1994, the U.S. Post Office issued a 32-cent stamp in Coleman's honor.

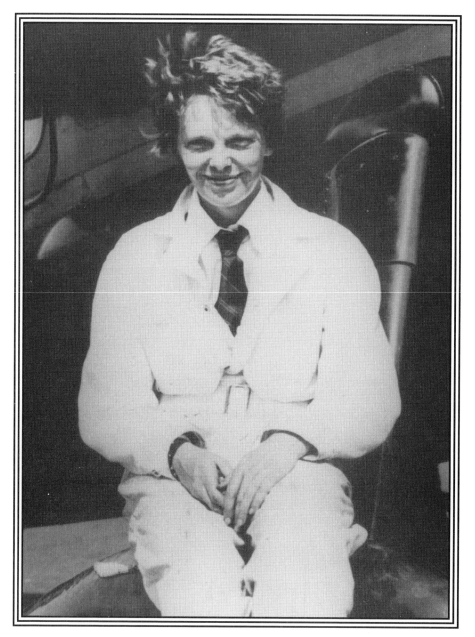

Amelia Earhart

3

Amelia Earhart
(1897–1937)

On July 2, 1937, Amelia Earhart and her navigator, Fred Noonan, took off from Lae, New Guinea. Lae is a small island in the Pacific Ocean. The two were on the last leg of their around-the-world flight. Their goal was Howland Island. This was a dangerous flight because they had to fly for a long stretch over water. The island of Lae was over 2,500 miles away. Unfortunately, the two would never be seen again. Their disappearance has become the most puzzling aviation mystery of all times.

Amelia Mary Earhart was born on July 24, 1897. Her parents, Amy Otis and Edwin Stanton Earhart, had one other daughter, Muriel, born two years later.

In 1916, Amelia graduated from Hyde Park High School in Chicago, Illinois. Her yearbook read, "The girl in brown who walks alone." [1]

During World War I, Earhart worked as a nurse's aide in a Toronto, Canada, military hospital. After the war, she thought she would like to become a doctor. In the fall of 1919, she enrolled in Columbia University's medical school. "It took me only a few months to discover that I probably should not make the ideal physician," she said. [2]

In 1920, her father brought her to her first airplane ride. It was at an air show in California. The open-cockpit biplane climbed into the sky. The pilot sat behind her. "As soon as we left the ground I knew I myself had to fly," said Amelia. [3] That evening she announced at dinner, "I think I'd like to learn to fly." [4] Her father replied, "Not a bad idea. When do you start?" Her flying lessons began in January 1921.

Even before she earned her license, Earhart began setting records. In October 1922, she set a women's altitude record of 14,000 feet. "In 1922 I certainly didn't think of my flying as a means to anything but having fun," [5] Earhart said. She earned her pilot's license on May 15, 1923.

Earhart's flying career was on again, off again. She had made attempts at medical school, taken a job as a social worker in Boston, and even taught English to immigrants. However, her passion for flying remained strong.

In 1927, the Atlantic Ocean was a major challenge for aviation. Flying across the Atlantic was unsafe. Charles Lindbergh had made the first solo crossing in May 1927. That year, nineteen others died in failed attempts. Three women were among the dead. They had been passengers of male pilots.

In 1928, Earhart's life took a new turn when George Putnam invited her to fly across the Atlantic. Putnam was a book publisher known for his ability to promote profitable book projects. He worked with Charles Lindbergh after he made his first flight over the Atlantic. Lindbergh's book about the flight, *We,* became a best-seller after it was published in 1927.

Since many thought Earhart resembled Charles Lindbergh, Putnam called her "Lady Lindy." Earhart and Putnam became good friends while the details were being worked out for the trip over the Atlantic.

Amy Phipps Guest of Pittsburgh, Pennsylvania, sponsored the trip. Guest purchased a Fokker trimotor airplane and named it the *Friendship*. Earhart would join the crew of the *Friendship*.

Just before the trip, the *Friendship's* wheels were replaced by pontoons, or portable floats. The pontoon-equipped plane was a significant part of the trip. This plane was different from the land planes previously used for the trip. The land planes would have to retrace their paths or risk a crash on some emergency field if trouble arose from weather conditions. However, the pontoon-equipped plane could be brought safely to water and could conserve fuel until a suitable landing could be found.[6]

The *Friendship* took off on June 17, 1928, with Earhart as a passenger. Earhart spent most of the flight wedged between two gas tanks. To use the time wisely, she kept a notebook of her personal observations that she later recorded in the book, *20 Hours, 40 Minutes.*

She watched the pilot as he flew through fog and rain. They flew through some of the worst storms in the north Atlantic. She studied his every move. During the long, cold, dangerous trip, they lost radio contact. They flew blind just 300 feet over the waves. They landed in Wales, in the British Isles, with about a gallon of fuel left. Earhart became the first woman to successfully fly across the Atlantic.

Friendship's pilot, Wilmer Stultz, received $20,000, and the navigator, Louis Gordon, $5,000. Earhart was not paid. "My own compensation which I had never really seriously considered was in addition to the fun of the exploit itself, the opportunities in aviation, writing and the like which the Atlantic crossing opened up."[7]

Earhart's fame grew and so did her relationship with George Putnam. After Putnam and his wife divorced, Earhart and Putnam were married on February 7, 1931. Earhart kept her maiden name professionally and seldom wore her wedding ring.

Putnam promoted his wife and financed her flying. He scheduled twenty-seven public

Amelia Earhart is greeted by 300,000 spectators in Boston after completing a cross-Atlantic flight. From left: Mayor Malcolm E. Nichols, navigator Lou Gordon, Earhart, and pilot Wilmer Stultz.

appearances in one month. The public wanted to hear about Earhart's risky crossing, and they wanted to see the physical resemblance to Lindbergh. She became the spokesperson for women in aviation. Her desire to see more women in aviation finally had a forum.

In August 1928, she took a job as an associate editor for *Cosmopolitan* magazine. She wrote articles on flying. One article was called, "Shall You Let Your Daughter Fly?" Her answer was a definite yes.

There was still the challenge of flying the Atlantic alone. This was something Earhart felt she had to do. "Ever since my first crossing in the *Friendship*, in 1928, when I was merely a passenger, I have wanted to attempt a solo flight," she said.[8]

On Friday, May 20, 1932, she took off alone from Harbor Grace, Newfoundland. Her goal was Ireland. Earhart flew through dangerous storms. There was an engine fire, and ice formed on the wings of her plane. Her instruments did not work properly, and she flew blind through an Atlantic storm.

Earhart had expected the flight would cover 1,860 miles. But because of bad weather and instrument problems, she flew 2,065 miles. In spite of the dangerous crossing, she landed safely. She had earned her reputation. She would be remembered forever. Earhart became the first woman to successfully fly alone across the Atlantic. She was only the second person in the world to accomplish this feat. She received a hero's welcome when she came home.

In 1935, Earhart set another aviation record. She flew from Honolulu, Hawaii, to Oakland, California, the longest overwater distance between two points. She became the first person to solo between those two points. Earhart received criticism from the media for her attempt because many thought it was purely a publicity stunt. However, Earhart ignored the criticism.

Earhart's next goal was to fly a true around-the-world flight. Because of the danger and the great distance, no one had flown around the world at the equator. Attempts had been made north of the equator, where there was mostly land and there were no long stretches of water. However, south of the equator was made up of water, and no one had attempted it. Earhart decided to make the trip.

Earhart's fame and efforts to increase opportunities for women in aviation resulted in her appointment as a consultant of careers for women at Purdue University. Her affiliation with Purdue prompted two members of the Purdue Research Foundation to donate money for Earhart to buy a twin-engine Lockheed Electra for her around-the-world flight.[9]

She began to prepare for what she said would be her last long-distance flight. In a letter she wrote to her husband and mailed during her last flight, she said, "Please know that I am quite aware of the hazards. I want to do it because I want to do it."[10]

Earhart planned to fly an east-to-west flight from California to Hawaii. She planned to fly from San Francisco to Hawaii, Australia, and India, across Africa to Brazil and on to New York. She would fly as close to the equator as possible. The distance was about 27,000 miles. On the first leg of the flight to Honolulu, there were no problems. On takeoff from Hawaii, a tire blew. The plane was heavily damaged and needed repairs. Earhart shipped it back by boat to California.

Fred Noonan, her navigator, studied the global weather conditions. He decided that they should make a second attempt on June 2, 1937. The trip went well for forty days. They had traveled 22,000 miles.

Before the last leg of the trip, Earhart began having problems with the fuel gauge and the electrical instruments. She took the plane in to be repaired. After the plane was thoroughly checked, everything that was not needed for the transpacific flight was packed away to be sent home. Some of the things taken off the plane included parachutes and some survival equipment.[11]

Then came the longest and most dangerous leg: a 2,556-mile hop from New Guinea to Howland Island. Howland Island is a one-mile-by-two-mile island near the equator. On board, they had enough fuel to stay airborne between twenty and twenty-one hours. Noonan estimated they would reach Howland in about 18 1/2 hours. Noonan had trouble picking up radio signals so he could not navigate accurately.

For Earhart's safety, the U.S. Navy had placed ships along the route. The U.S. Coast Guard cutter *Itasca* served as the radio contact and was waiting with supplies off the coast of Howland Island where they were expected to land.

Earhart sent several messages en route to Howland Island, but the plane never arrived. The last message received from her read, "We are on the line of position 157-337 . . . We are running north and south." The message was too short. No one could pinpoint her position.

Officials knew she had missed the small speck of an island. They also knew she would soon run out of fuel. However, something troubled them even more. They discovered that Earhart had removed some radio equipment. She wanted to reduce the plane's weight. The aircraft also did not have an emergency radio.

An investigation by the U.S. Navy found that Earhart and Noonan did not understand how to operate the radios correctly. The report said the two also did not know about other radio frequencies available. If they had, they could have possibly given better information about their position.

President Franklin D. Roosevelt ordered a huge 260,000-square-mile air-sea search. It never turned up any trace of the plane or the crew. On July 18, 1937, the Navy declared the two lost at sea.

Earhart's disappearance still raises theories. Some say she was a spy for the United States and executed by the Japanese because she had seen their military buildup in the Pacific. Another says she simply ran out of fuel and crashed into the sea.

Some said she was not qualified to make the flight. However, her record speaks for itself. She was the first to fly across the country in an autogiro, an early helicopter-like aircraft. She was the first person to fly solo from Hawaii to California. She was the first person to solo from Mexico to Newark, New Jersey. As a writer, she made millions of friends for aviation. As a public speaker, she influenced women in positive ways.

Earhart fought for women's rights. Her involvement in aviation showed women new possibilities. She is a great role model for women. Her writing reinforced her belief that a woman can do anything she sets her mind to.

Earhart wrote to her husband, George Putnam, "Women must try to do things as men have tried. When they fail, their failure must be but a challenge to others."[12]

On July 24, 1963, the U.S. Post Office issued an eight-cent airmail stamp in Amelia Earhart's honor.

Anne Morrow Lindbergh
(1906–2001)

Anne Morrow Lindbergh was born June 22, 1906, in Englewood, New Jersey. She was the daughter of ambassador Dwight Morrow. Her mother, Elizabeth Cutter Morrow, was a poet and a promoter of women's education. Anne grew up in wealthy surroundings. The family spent summers at the seashore in Martha's Vineyard in Cape Cod. Anne wanted to be a writer and went to Smith College to study literature. She received a bachelor of arts degree in literature in 1928.

Anne Morrow was an author, pilot, and mother of six children. When she was fourteen years old, she wrote in the school paper that she wanted to marry a hero. Nine years later, she married a hero, the

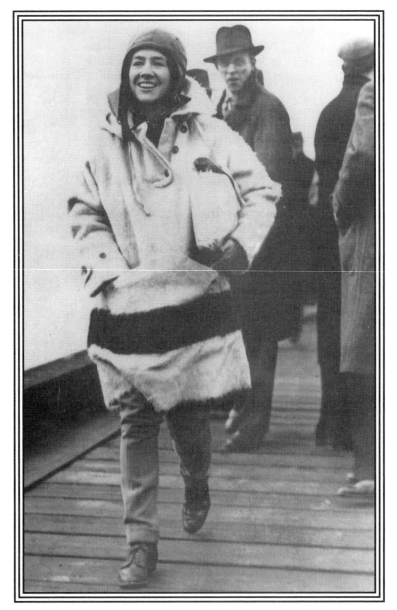

Anne Morrow Lindbergh

world-famous aviator Charles A. Lindbergh, Jr. He was the first man to fly solo across the Atlantic Ocean.

Soon after his famous flight, Charles Lindbergh was invited to visit the Morrows in Mexico. Dwight Morrow was the ambassador for the United States. Charles was attracted to Anne by her quiet, contemplative personality. Anne wondered what it would be like to be married to the most famous person in the world. On their first date, he took her for her first airplane ride.[1] Charles often took Anne flying during their courtship, and he soon taught her to fly. They began to correspond regularly as well. Within a short time, they were engaged and planned a secret wedding. Anne Morrow married Charles A. Lindbergh, Jr., on May 27, 1929.

After she married Charles, her life changed forever. She quickly adopted her husband's aviation goals. In the first year and a half of their marriage, the couple made eight transcontinental survey flights for Transcontinental Air Transport (TWA).[2] These flights mapped possible air routes for the airlines. They made air surveys across the United States and the Caribbean. These routes were later used for airmail service. During these early flights, Anne served as Charles' copilot, navigator, and radio operator in a Lockheed Sirius. The plane is now on display in the Pioneers of Flight Gallery of the National Air and Space Museum in Washington D.C. Even though Anne earned her fame through her marriage to Charles Lindbergh, she established her own career as a pilot.

In January 1930, Anne became the first woman to be licensed as a glider pilot. That same year, she and Charles set a transcontinental speed record by flying from Los Angeles to New York in less than fifteen hours.[3] Anne acted as her husband's copilot and navigator. At the time, she was seven months pregnant. Although the route was surrounded by storms and she was sick most of the trip, she continued providing Charles with navigation data.

In 1931, she received her private pilot's license. Charles served as both her mentor and her flight instructor. Hundreds of newspapermen hounded the couple.

In 1931, the couple flew a single-engine airplane over dangerous and unmapped routes. They mapped out the routes for airlines and airmail service. Those routes stretched from Canada and Alaska to Japan and China. Anne used her training as a writer to write about this adventure in her first book, *North to the Orient*. In this book, she described her amazement with life from the air. "For not only is life put into new patterns from the air, but it is somehow arrested, frozen into form . . . A glaze is put over life. There is no flaw, no crack in the surface; a still reservoir, no ripple on its face."[4]

Anne endured the difficult conditions during flights across unforgiving and hazardous terrain. She suffered many physical hardships. Often she and

Charles slept in their airplane. In flight, the cabin temperature sometimes dropped below zero. She worked hard to keep the equipment working in the harsh environment. She worked even harder as the radio operator and copilot.

Anne accompanied Charles on his flights in the United States. She was like a goodwill ambassador. Charles was shy, so she greeted the crowds with skillfulness and smiles.

Charles Lindbergh had been Pan American Airways' technical advisor. In 1933, the couple made a transatlantic flight. They were studying possible Atlantic air routes. After the flight, the Lindberghs toured Europe. They flew to Moscow and down the West Coast of Africa. They were exposed to many foreign cultures. Anne again acted as a goodwill ambassador. She always made friends with the local people and answered their questions.

Throughout these years of flying and exploring, she became a mother. As a mother, Anne was the happiest. In 1932, her happiness turned to sorrow. Her firstborn son, Charles Lindbergh III, was kidnapped and murdered. Anne fell into a deep depression.

In 1933, Anne was pregnant with their second child. She completed a five-and-a-half-month, 30,000-mile survey of the North and South Atlantic air routes with Charles. She wrote of their trip in *Listen! The Wind.* Charles called this trip more difficult and hazardous than his New York-to-Paris flight in 1927.

After the birth of her second son, Jon, the Lindbergh's other children, Land, Anne, Scott, and Reeve soon followed. The Lindberghs continued their flying. As a true working partner, Anne often referred to herself as "Charles' faithful page." Her husband in turn said, "No woman exists or has existed who is her equal."

However, Anne's marriage to Charles was difficult. He wanted his wife to be his flying companion. He also had a strong desire to pursue specific goals in aviation and lived for the adventure of flying. When he had an opportunity to fly, he would ask Anne to join him. Many times their trips took them away from the children for long periods of time. Anne felt uneasy about leaving her children, so she decided to stop flying and concentrate more on her roles as a mother and a writer. Her writing and her children became her fulfillment.[5]

One of Anne's most successful books was inspired by several vacations she and Charles spent on the Sanibel Island beach in Florida. The couple took many long walks on the beach. While walking, she studied the seashells that washed up on the beach and compared the different shells to love, marriage, youth, and old age. She wrote a book from her experiences entitled, *A Gift From the Sea* which became a best-seller. In the book, she advised women to free themselves from the daily routines of life and seek self-fulfillment.

Anne Morrow Lindbergh earned her own measure of fame by accompanying husband Charles on his aviation adventures during the 1930s.

Although Anne Morrow Lindbergh had walked away from flying, flying still remained a fascination. She said, "Security in a relationship lies neither in looking back to what it was in nostalgia, nor forward to what it might be in dread or anticipation, but living in the present relationship and accepting it as it is now."[6] This seems to be exactly how she lived her life.

In 1933, Anne Lindbergh was recognized for her pioneering roles on the transatlantic flights with Charles. She received the United States Flag Association Cross of Honor. A year later, the National Geographic Society awarded her the Hubbard Gold Medal. It honored her 40,000 miles of flying over five continents. She was the first woman to receive this award. Only nine men including her husband had won this medal.

During her life, Anne Lindbergh earned many honors and awards. She earned honorary degrees from four colleges. She was inducted into the National Aviation Hall of Fame, the National Women's Hall of Fame, and the Aviation Hall of Fame of New Jersey. She also received the Christopher Award for the fifth volume of her diaries, *War Within and Without*.

Anne Lindbergh wrote more than thirteen major works. In *Earth Shine*, she wrote of being at Cape Kennedy for the first moon-orbiting flight. She wrote that the photographs of Earth that *Apollo 8* brought back gave humankind "a new sense of Earth's richness and beauty." In the novel, *The Steep*

Ascent, she tells the story of a dangerous flight made by a husband and wife team.

Anne Lindbergh wrote, "And I was conscious again of the fundamental magic of flying, a miracle that has nothing to do with any of its practical purposes—purposes of speed, accessibility, and convenience—and will not change as they change . . ."[7]

Anne Lindbergh died February 7, 2001 at the age of 94.

Jacqueline Cochran

Jacqueline Cochran
(1910 ?–1980)

Jacqueline (Jackie) Cochran was an American hero. She was also one of the most influential women of the twentieth century. Cochran was the first woman to fly a bomber across the Atlantic Ocean to England. She was the first woman to fly a jet across the Atlantic and the first woman to break the sound barrier.

Her aviation career spanned more than forty years. When she died in 1980, Jackie Cochran held more speed, altitude, and distance records than any pilot, male or female. She was called "the greatest woman pilot in aviation history."[1]

There are no accurate records of when Cochran was born. Most people think it was around 1910. Her parents died when she was an infant.[2] She never knew her real name or her real birthday. She grew up as a foster child in a poor family.

Jackie Cochran went without shoes until she was eight years old and wore cast-off flour sacks for clothes when she went to work in a sawmill.

Her bed was a mat on the floor. Her diet was usually fish, pork bellies, and black-eyed peas. Sometimes, she searched in the woods and fields for pinecone nuts. Later she picked her name, Jacqueline Cochran, from a Pensacola phone book.[3]

Everyone in Cochran's family worked. Her foster father and two foster brothers worked in a sawmill. They were paid in wood chips for their labor. The chips were like money, but good only at the company's store. There were never enough chips to meet the week's expenses.

At age ten, Jackie Cochran was earning six cents an hour for a twelve-hour shift. She supervised fifteen other children in a Georgia cotton mill. During an employee strike, she found work in a beauty shop. This experience would change her life forever.

Cochran was hired by a beauty shop owner. By the time she was thirteen, she knew how to give a professional haircut. She also mastered the newly invented permanent wave.[4] One of the customers in the shop encouraged Cochran to do something more serious with her life.[5]

She decided to enroll in nursing school. She had saved enough money to complete the required three years of training. However, formal schooling did not come easy to Cochran. "I learned my ABCs by studying the letters on the boxcars," she said, "and began to figure out the words."[6]

Cochran studied nursing at a hospital in Alabama. Later she went to work for a country doctor in Florida. Nursing barely paid her enough to live on. It was also depressing. One day she delivered a baby by an oil lamp in a shack. She discovered the family did not even have a piece of cloth to wrap around the infant. Cochran knew then that she did not want to be a nurse.

After quitting nursing, Cochran returned to work in a Pensacola beauty shop. When she had saved enough money, she bought a half interest in the beauty shop. After helping to build the business, she sold her half of the business and went to New York City.

The year was 1929. The stock market had crashed and thousands of people were out of work. It was almost impossible for anyone to find a job. Again, Jackie was determined. She walked into the Saks Fifth Avenue beauty shop. After thirty minutes, she had talked them into hiring her.

In 1932, Cochran was having dinner in a Miami restaurant. Seated alongside her was a Wall Street millionaire named Floyd Odlum. They struck up a conversation, and she shared with him her dream to open her own cosmetics business.

Odlum pointed out that the Depression had made every business very competitive. She would need wings to keep up with her competition, he said.

Cochran took his comment seriously. It was the summer of 1932. Crowds were cheering Amelia Earhart's solo flight across the Atlantic. Cochran went to Roosevelt Field, on Long Island, to begin flying lessons. She soloed in three days. She had the same determination that helped her survive the sawmills in Florida. She passed her pilot license exam two weeks later. She said later, "When I paid for my first lesson, the beauty operator ceased to exist and an aviator was born." [7]

Women pilots of the 1930s were a special group. Most were born wealthy. "I had not been born to such surroundings," said Cochran. "But if I had to push my way in and push my way to the top I'd do it." [8]

Within two years, she had established Jacqueline Cochran Cosmetics. She had a salon in Chicago and a cosmetics laboratory in New Jersey. She had product outlets throughout the United States. Her cosmetics business was making money. She used the income to support her first love, flying.

In the early 1930s, flying was still dangerous. Only a few thousand men and a few hundred women had pilot's licenses. "The reason I went for record breaking and long-distance flying," said Cochran, "was simply then as now, the jobs as test pilots and airline pilots went to men, not women. The chances were that if a woman was selected for this training, before she had returned a profit on the heavy investment in such training, she would have converted herself into a wife and mother and stopped working."[9]

She continued, "I had a choice between piloting light machines which were boring and cost money, or getting hold of fast, up-to-date aircraft in which I could try to break records. I might risk my neck but I could probably earn a living."[10]

In 1936, Cochran married Floyd Odlum. Cochran was becoming a legend in aviation. In 1937, she set three speed records. In 1939, she set an altitude record of 33,000 feet.

By 1941, Cochran had set seventeen aviation records. In 1942, The British Air Transport Auxiliary needed qualified pilots to ferry planes. Cochran was asked to recruit some experienced women pilots and go to England. Cochran and twenty-seven women pilots went to England to ferry military aircraft from factories to air bases in England.

Cochran returned to the United States to help form the Women Airforce Service Pilots (WASP). The WASP was a group of about one-thousand civilian women pilots. They flew fighters and bombers from factories to air bases in the United States. This freed up male pilots for combat flying. This was also a dangerous type of flying. The airplanes had just rolled off the assembly line and had not been tested. The WASP members were like test pilots.

By the early 1950s, jet fighters were on the scene. Cochran wanted to fly one. Chuck Yeager, the first person to break the sound barrier, prepared Jackie for

Jacqueline Cochran was one of the most famous female fliers in the 1930s.

the dangerous flight. It cost one-million dollars per flight hour for insurance. In May 1953, Cochran became the first woman to fly at supersonic speeds. Supersonic speeds are considered above the speed of sound, which is about 650 miles per hour. In six hours of flying, Cochran made thirteen flights. She broke the sound barrier three times. In her first dive from 47,000 feet, she failed to break the sound barrier.

Cochran would not give up. She refueled and went up again. This time she broke the sound barrier. Then, to satisfy the news media, she did it again. In a nearly vertical dive from 50,000 feet, Cochran and Yeager rocketed downward at full throttle. Cochran later said it was a spiritual and emotional experience that left her speechless. On June 6, 1960, she became the first woman to fly at twice the speed of sound.

Cochran received many aviation and business awards. In 1945, she received the Distinguished Service Medal once, and the Distinguished Flying Cross three times. This was an honor generally awarded only to military personnel. She won the International Harmon Trophy fourteen times. She rose to the rank of colonel in the Air Force Reserve. Cochran received the gold wings of the Federation Aeronautique International and honorary wings from half a dozen air forces. She earned the French Legion of Honor, several honorary degrees, and the "Woman of the Year" award in 1953 and 1954. In 1954, she wrote her autobiography, *The Stars at*

Noon. In her early sixties, she became the first woman to pilot a jet across the Atlantic.

In her mid-sixties, a pacemaker forced her to give up flying. A pacemaker is a device that produces electric pulses similar to a heart beat.

After her husband died in 1977, her health began to fail. Heart and kidney disease confined her to a wheelchair. She had been a friend to four presidents and dozens of European royalty. She died August 7, 1980.

On March 9, 1996, the U.S. Postal Service issued a fifty-cent airmail stamp honoring Jackie Cochran.

Betty Skelton Frankman
(1926–)

Betty Skelton holds more combined aviation and automotive records that anyone in history. She was the first woman to cut a ribbon while flying inverted. Skelton piloted the smallest plane, a Pitts Special, to cross the Irish Sea. She also set two world light-plane altitude records. The highest was 29,050 feet in a Piper Cub in 1951.

Betty was born on June 28, 1926 in Pensacola, Florida, to David and Myrtle Skelton. As a young girl, she would watch the Navy biplanes fly their aerobatic routines over her backyard. Aerobatics are unusual flying maneuvers such as rolls, loops, dives, and inverted flying. She dreamed one day she would fly.

Betty recalls playing with model airplanes instead of dolls. She wanted to fly so badly; she soloed

Betty Skelton Frankman

illegally at the age of twelve. She repeated her solo flight at the legal age of sixteen. A commercial pilot at age eighteen and a flight instructor at nineteen, Betty was on her way to the stars.

Betty's real wish was to fly military planes as a ferry pilot in the Women Airforce Service Pilots (WASP) program. Created during World War II, the WASP was a group of about one-thousand civilian women pilots. They flew new fighters and bombers from factories to the air bases around the United States. Skelton had the necessary flight experience, but she was only seventeen. The minimum age was eighteen and a half. The WASP program ended four months before she reached the right age. During this time, she met Clem Whittenbeck, a famous aerobatic pilot of the 1930s. He taught Betty how to fly loops, rolls, and inverted flying.

"My first aerobatic biplane, a *Great Lakes*, was a real crate!" said Frankman. "I found it behind a hangar. It was in bad shape. It had crashed and was in pieces. It was not nearly as manageable as a true aerobatic plane should be."[1] With help, Betty rebuilt the airplane. She had her share of narrow escapes in the old biplane. She even crashed it once. Frankman flew her first professional air show in 1946 in Jacksonville, Florida. She earned twenty-five dollars for the performance.[2]

In 1948, Frankman saw a new experimental biplane called the Pitts Special. It was a single-seat, open cockpit aircraft. It weighed only 544 pounds.

It was only 14 feet 8 inches long and had a 15-foot 3-inch wingspan. It was about the size of a car. At the time, it was the smallest airplane in the world. This was the plane she wanted to fly.

Eventually she bought the plane. At the time, she did not know that she and the airplane would become a famous team. Her airplane would become the most famous aerobatic aircraft in the world. Frankman would teach the little Pitts Special many new maneuvers. The airplane also taught Frankman a lesson.

She flew her new airplane back to her home base in Tampa, Florida. A large crowd of friends had gathered to welcome Frankman. Her landing was smooth. As she brought the airplane to a stop, it went out of control. "At low speeds, the rudder was less effective due to less air flow over the area," said Frankman. "Only the brakes would keep me going straight."[3] As she tried to bring the plane under control she said under her breath "You little stinker!" The little Pitts Special did not like the remark and "ground looped." A ground loop is a sharp uncontrollable turn on the ground. Frankman stopped the airplane and was not hurt. However, from that moment on they would live forever as Betty Skelton and her *Little Stinker*.

To become a champion, Frankman would practice for hours. Sometimes she spent hours on just one maneuver. During practice, she placed towels between herself and the safety harnesses to act as cushions.

Nevertheless, they never got rid of all the pressure. As a result, Frankman was always bruised. Some of her maneuvers forced blood to her face. Sometimes, she would go for weeks with black eyes and blotches on her face. During other maneuvers, the blood would drain from her head. She would sometimes experience a red out, a short loss of consciousness.

When Frankman decided to fly *Little Stinker*, she quietly shared her beliefs and expectations with her little friend. "If we are to fly together we must think and believe as one . . . you must believe in yourself. Let your free spirit take you where you will, and when it falters, let your soul demand that you not give up, but only aspire to climb higher and higher."[4]

Soon Frankman and *Little Stinker* worked as one. Her movements transmitted calm and confidence to the airplane. Her little friend reacted as an extension of Frankman's body. *Little Stinker* rolled and looped to her every command.

The maneuver Frankman is best known for is the inverted ribbon cut. This involves flying inverted and cutting a ribbon strung between two poles, ten feet from the ground. Her friends tried to talk her out of it. They said it was too dangerous.

Frankman promised her friends she would practice until she felt comfortable. Her first pass was deliberately high but right on target. Feeling confident, she set up to cut the ribbon on her second try. Just as she rolled inverted, the engine quit. She was less than ten feet above the ground.

Frankman had built a 10 percent safety rule into her routine. She always allowed herself 10 percent more airspeed than she needed. When possible, she allowed 10 percent more altitude than she needed. Frankman's 10 percent rule saved her life that day. The extra airspeed allowed her to roll over and land safely.

Frankman worked twice as hard as everyone else did. "It is not easy to be the best," she told her *Little Stinker.* "You must have the courage to bear pain, disappointment, and heartbreak. You must learn how to face danger and understand fear, yet not be afraid. You must establish your goal, and . . . in your every waking moment you must say to yourself, 'I can do it.'"[5]

Aerobatic flying is dangerous and sometimes fatal. "One of the hardest things about flying the aerobatic circuit was enduring the pain of watching friends die," she said. "At times it felt like a waiting game. I wondered who would be next." Frankman looked on death as one of the risks of the business. "Learning to fear death without actually being afraid was something you had to do to make it through."[6]

As a champion, Frankman was always in demand, but it was hard for a woman to earn money in the sport she loved so much. Flying was expensive, and there was not much chance for a woman to advance in aviation back then. If she stayed in aviation, she would have to go back to being a flight instructor. This was hardly a challenge for her.

Betty Skelton Frankman nicknamed her plane "Little Stinker." It was an airplane the size of a small car.

On October 2, 1951, at the age of twenty-six, Frankman retired from professional acrobatic flying.

Betty Skelton Frankman changed how women were seen in competitive aerobatics. In those days, the rules said women were not allowed to compete with the men. She challenged the Professional Race Pilots Association's rules. They made changes, and today women can race with the men.

Frankman's philosophy was simple. "Real champions never look back, but only forward in search of new and more worthwhile challenges."[7] Frankman loved speed, so her next career was in auto racing. Her records in this field are as exciting as those in her aviation career. She became the first woman hired as a test driver in the auto industry. Frankman broke the world land speed record for women four times. She became the first woman to drive a jet-powered car over 300 miles per hour (315.72 to be exact). She won nine sport car records for speed and acceleration. She was also the first woman to drive an Indianapolis race car.

"I have always been interested in speed," she said. "It's pretty fortunate when you can find something you love to do so much and it is also your occupation."[8]

Frankman says her career successes came from having, "the coolness of a champion bullfighter, the fighting spirit of a cornered cobra, and the dedication of a priest."[9]

One of Frankman's most exciting firsts came in 1959. She became the first woman to take the astronaut tests with National Aeronautics and Space Administration (NASA). These were the same tests given to the original seven male *Mercury* astronauts.

"We were exploring the possibilities of women being included in the space program," said Frankman. "I wanted to influence NASA that women should be included in their program."[10]

Frankman spent four months going through the tests. "Everyone was polite, helpful and friendly," she said. "But it didn't take me long to learn that it might take a gal a lifetime to penetrate NASA's 'space wall.'"[11]

Frankman met the seven *Mercury* astronauts. "Learning about their challenges and equipment resulted in the most soul searching experience of my life. I was honored to have even a tiny part of it. No human had ever been in space!"[12]

Look magazine ran a cover story on Frankman's tests on February 2, 1960. The story created an outcry from women pilots. They wanted to become astronauts, too. NASA picked thirteen women to take the tests. They all passed the tests, but none ever went into space. "I had estimated it was going to take twenty to twenty-five years for a woman pilot to break the barrier," said Frankman.[13] She was right. The first American woman to fly into space was Sally Ride in June 1983.

Betty Skelton Frankman earned dozens of awards and honors. She won the International Feminine Aerobatic Championship three consecutive years— 1948, 1949, and 1950. She received honorary wings from the United States Navy. There is also a trophy named for her: The Betty Skelton First Lady of Aerobatics Award. Each year the woman pilot with the highest score at the U.S. National Aerobatic Competition wins this award.

Little Stinker is now in the Smithsonian's Air and Space Museum. "It is tremendously gratifying to know that children may see the tiny plane for decades to come. Hopefully it will inspire some to seek a future in the sky and space," said Frankman.[14]

7

Bonnie Tiburzi

(1948–)

In 1973, Bonnie Tiburzi became the first female pilot hired by a major airline. She was hired by American Airlines. Bonnie's grandfather had been the first man in Sweden to manufacture aircraft parts. Her father was a pilot during World War II with the Air Transport Command and TWA. After the war, he opened a flight school in Danbury, Connecticut. Bonnie's first flying lessons were on her father's lap. By the time she was twelve, she knew how to read the instruments on an airplane.

"I used to hang around the hangars and airport after school and on weekends," she said. "To me the hangars and airstrip were an extension of our house."[1]

Bonnie Tiburzi

Bonnie had school friends growing up, but the mechanics and pilots were her best friends. "I liked them better than anyone else I knew."[2]

When Bonnie was fourteen, her father closed his business and moved his family to Florida. She joined the tennis team at her new high school and made the honor roll during the tennis season. Her new friends were her classmates. They would go to the beach after school, not the airport. Surfing, not flying, became the center of her world, but not for long.

"I missed the airplanes . . . my life was filled with the idea of flying. It was what real people did."[3]

As a teenager in the sixties, people began to ask Bonnie what she planned to do when she grew up. "I'm going to be an airline pilot, just like my father was," she would reply. [4]

However, there were no women pilots flying for the airlines then. She saw no reason why they did not. There were plenty of women pilots. The people she shared this dream with thought she would eventually change her mind.

In 1967, when Bonnie graduated high school, she still dreamed of being an airline pilot. She had wondered often about what she wanted to do with her life. She thought about being a dancer, a teacher, and even a veterinarian. She also still dreamed about being an airline pilot.

Since she did not want to go to college, Bonnie and her parents decided she should go to France. They arranged through an exchange agency for her to live with a French family. She would get a room and meals and French lessons. Bonnie quickly discovered this was not for her. The family preferred English. She soon found a family with three children who only spoke French and needed a nanny.

By Christmas 1968, Bonnie Tiburzi was back home in Florida. If she wanted to be an airline pilot, she would have to learn the technical side of flying, so she enrolled in college in northern Florida.

In the summer of 1969, she took the first big step toward her goal. She soloed and earned her student pilot certificate. That is like a learner's permit for a car. The next step was getting her pilot's license.

Bonnie went to work at her father's travel agency in Florida. Now with a steady income, she began to take her flying lessons seriously. Eight months later, she had her private pilot's license. Now she could see a whole set of goals before her. She would need a commercial pilot's license and then an airline transport pilot's license. These required additional school lessons and flying time. She began ferrying small planes around south Florida to build her flight time.

In early 1970, Bonnie went to Europe to gain more flying experience. She found a job as a copilot for a charter company. The winter weather in Europe became one snowstorm after another. Because of the bad weather, Bonnie did not fly much, so she decided to return to Florida. In January 1971, she passed her commercial flying exam. She needed one more license, her airline transport pilot rating. Then she could apply to the airlines.

Bonnie Tiburzi was fortunate growing up. She was not surrounded by negative influences. "I always wanted to be an airline pilot and my parents never told me I couldn't," she said.[5] "One of my first jobs was with a small commuter in Florida, flying a DC-3. We specialized in charter flights for sport fishermen. In those days, a few passengers had doubts about my ability. Some would ask did I know how to get off the runway."[6]

"I once flew a famous baseball star (Ted Williams) who demanded to see my license. Then he sat up front the whole trip and kept asking was I sure I could fly. He was a pilot during the war and had never seen a woman fly."[7]

By the spring of 1972, Tiburzi was becoming discouraged. She had more than a thousand hours of flying time, but she was no closer to her goal of becoming an airline pilot. She had been giving flying lessons, and some of her students had gone off to get jobs with the airlines.

She began to send out applications and asked some airline pilots how they got their jobs. Most of them said that they had been ex-military pilots. Her brother Allan, an airline pilot on the DC-8 for Seaboard World Airlines even said, "They're not going to hire a woman. That's a man's job, and men need those jobs. They have to support their families."[8]

She could hardly believe the words coming from her own brother. He later changed his mind.

The airlines sometimes responded to her applications by sending her information. They also mentioned they had a waiting list of pilots to be hired.

Then something happened. It would trigger a chain of events Tiburzi could never have dreamed of. *Harper's Bazaar* was planning a Florida issue for their January 1973 magazine. Tiburzi would be one of the feature stories. The story headline read "Bonnie Tiburzi: In Control." It described her as "—A dynamic woman . . . with a commercial pilot's rating. Only one major obstacle in her way . . . The commercial airlines will only accept a woman as an attractive order taker for 'coffee, tea or milk.' Bonnie aims to change all that and be the first woman in the cockpit."[9]

Gene Steele, a lawyer with the Federal Aviation Administration (FAA), saw the article and called her. At first, Tiburzi thought she had violated some FAA regulation. "American's hiring," he said.[10]

She told him she had applied to American Airlines, but they had not answered. He told her that she had to keep updating her application so they could keep updated on what she was doing.

Tiburzi wrote to the employment office of American Airlines. She informed them that she had over fourteen-hundred flying hours.

Within two weeks, things began to happen. American Airlines invited her to their office for an in-person interview and some tests.[11]

The airline was friendly, and Tiburzi felt she did well on all the tests. However, she went home wondering. She thought her odds were about fifteen-thousand-to-one that she would be hired.

A few weeks later, at ten o'clock in the evening, the doorbell rang. Tiburzi knew it was the telegram. Was it a yes or a no from American Airlines? "Congratulations . . . Report for class March 30, 1973."[12]

After completing her training, Tiburzi became the first female flight engineer in the world. That was on the Boeing 727 jet. The flight engineer is a pilot who monitors all the important instruments on the jet. In time, she would pass the test for copilot, and then captain.

"Being the first woman hired by a major airline was great fun in the beginning," she said. "I was single and having a great time."[13]

"Most of the pilots were wonderful and supportive," she said. Some, however, treated her as a trespasser. The airline gave her a strength test. "Did they think I was going to carry the airplane across the country?"[14] she remarked. The pilots tested her in other ways. Once they put ten-pound weights in her flight bag and watched to see if she would use the "wimp wheels" to pull her bag behind her. She did not.

There was also some hostility, but not from the pilots. Some people said she was taking a job away from a man. Others said she was trying to "make a statement." In response to that, Bonnie said, "I'm

Bonnie Tiburzi as first officer on a Boeing 727.

not trying to make a statement, I'm just trying to make a living."[15]

She worried about her first day on the job. "I dreaded arriving in Chicago. The crew lounges at the airport were segregated by sex. I wondered what I was going to do when the captain and copilot headed for the lounge bearing the sign Male Crew Members Only, and the flight attendants went off to their own lounge.

"Deep in my heart I knew where I wanted to go. I belonged with the pilots, having earned the job of first officer. However, in terms of being a woman, it was awkward."[16]

"I headed for the male crew lounge, knowing that virtually all company personnel would know that I had arrived and were expecting me to show up at . . . well, wherever."[17]

"There it was. A sign, in big, bold black letters. male crew members only. It looked very crisp and forbidding."[18]

"Except that beneath it," said Bonnie, "penciled in equally bold lettering, were the added words: and Bonnie too!"[19]

When asked why she flies, Tiburzi's eyes widen, and her mouth breaks into a wide smile. "The joy of this achievement is insurmountable. In the early days, women pilots faced issues like whether we should wear skirts or pants, a blouse or shirt or a different hat. Today there are so many more important issues, like whether to fly when pregnant, or how to blend a family and flying, and a career."[20]

Bonnie Tiburzi likes to remind young women who dream of flying, "If you are determined, confident and committed, you'll do fine. You have to be good."[21]

Tiburzi received several aviation awards during her career. In 1974, she earned the Amita Award for the outstanding Italian American of the year. In 1980, she received the Amelia Earhart Award.

Tiburzi retired from American Airlines on August 31, 1998. She was a captain on the Boeing 757 and 767. "I wanted to change the balance in my life. I wanted to set some new priorities. After 26 years with American I retired to become a wife and mother."[22] Today Tiburzi and her husband raise their two children, Tony and Britt. In her off time, she is a board member of the College of Aeronautics in New York. She is also writing a book.

Nelda K. Lee
(1946–)

Nelda Lee was born September 14, 1946. She was the oldest of four children born to Horace and Faye Lee. As a youngster, she would look up from her farm in Alabama and watch the white trails of a high-flying aircraft. The thought of becoming a pilot never occurred to her. There were no family members in aviation, and her family could also not afford the expensive flying lessons. Being a pilot was just not one of the realistic possibilities for her when she grew up.

Her father's pilot friend gave Nelda her first airplane ride. She was four years old. She does not remember how she felt about it then. Her father, his friend, and Nelda went flying often. She feels now

Nelda Lee

perhaps it was those flights that planted the idea in her mind.

Her father was an engineer and she followed his example. She attended Auburn University, as he did. It was the late 1960s during the great space race between Russia and the United States. She majored in aerospace engineering. At the time, she was the only woman in the program. She was also only the second woman ever to enroll in the major at the school.

Nelda had always been fascinated with mechanical things. She had helped her father fix hundreds of things around their three-hundred-acre farm.

Once in college she thought that learning to fly would help her with her schoolwork. However, at the time, there were no flying courses in her curriculum at school. She had an idea. She approached the school officials and suggested she take flying as a four-hour elective course. "I told them that I thought my education would be more complete. They agreed!"[1]

Soon she was at the controls of a light airplane. Nelda Lee earned her fixed wing license in April 1969, when she was a senior at Auburn University. After she graduated, she joined McDonnell Aircraft as an associate engineer.

Lee's attraction to flight progressed through helicopters. "I was fascinated with how helicopters work," she said. "Mechanically they are so complex. I never thought I would fly one. I looked at helicopters the way a little girl looks at a new bicycle. I wondered what it would feel like to fly one."[2]

"One day a friend took me on a ride. I fell in love with helicopters. I told her I would never be able to afford the lessons. That is when she told me about the Doris Mullen Scholarship. It was offered by the Whirly-Girls, an international organization of women helicopter pilots. I applied for it. To my delightful surprise I won!"

Lee approached helicopter flying as an engineer. "I had studied helicopters in college and understood how they worked mechanically. I wanted to experience putting that knowledge to the actual test. It looked like something that would be both challenging and fun to do."[3]

Lee earned her helicopter license in 1977. She was one of only 247 female helicopter pilots in the world.[4] Today there are about 1,200 women helicopter pilots in the Whirly-Girls International Women Helicopter Pilots association.

Nelda Lee was the first woman to become a flight test engineer with her company. "As a licensed pilot, I set career goals to include a broad outlook. I wanted to be a flight test engineering team member."[5] Lee works at Boeing's aerospace tactical aircraft and missile systems operation. Today she is a principle engineer and manager of the tactical aircraft flight and ground test-engineering programs. She is responsible for more than sixty engineers, technicians, and researchers who work with engineers at Air Force and Navy bases.

Lee says her greatest flight took place in 1978. As an F-15 flight test engineer, Lee had an opportunity to ride in the backseat of the fighter jet. She was on the flight testing engineering team. Since she was an experienced licensed pilot, she was given the opportunity to fly the airplane:

Again, I approached it as a learning experience. I knew the airplane on paper, and had flown it in the simulator. Nothing prepared me for the thrill of actually flying the airplane.

I was strapped into the ejection seat. There was a harness around my shoulders, and straps on my thighs. I felt like I was part of the airplane.

The pilot pushed the throttles forward. The power I felt coming from the engines was awesome. The twin jet engines were practically screaming. The plane shot forward like a bullet. In less time than it takes to read this sentence, I was traveling at more than 300 miles per hour.

I was rocketing into the sky. I felt a giant, invisible hand pushing me back against my seat. About a minute later, we leveled off at 12,000 feet. The F-15 is a ride you will never find in an amusement park.

The pilot let me take the controls. He said, "It is easy to fly. Just think—turn left."

It was amazing. This aircraft weighs 45,000 pounds. I did as he said, and found myself very gently moving the control stick to the left. It was almost like steering a bicycle.

One of Lee's most satisfying moments was in 1991. The F-15 received wonderful comments from the allied pilots during Operation Desert Storm. She was proud of the job her team had done.

With thirty-three years as an aerospace engineer, Lee says she made a great career choice. At the time, she did not look at herself as a trailblazer in a male field. She also has never let being a woman limit her ability to improve. "I have never gone into a situation with the attitude that my gender was going to hold me back. I've had to prove myself—everyone does—but acceptance has never been a problem. Being one of a kind has always been fine with me."

For relaxation, Nelda likes to fly a helicopter. "Helicopters fascinate me." She says, "Flying is something I always wanted to do and helicopters are so much fun."

Nelda Lee's logical engineering mind also has a funny side. She went to a local community college and took several courses in face painting and clowning. Now she clowns around with "Plane Jane" and "Ethel Eggbeater." Dressed in a clown suit complete with goggles and leather flying helmet, she entertains at schools.

Along with special recognition for being the first woman to take the controls and fly the F-15 Eagle, Nelda Lee has earned more than a dozen awards and honors over the years. In 1988, she earned the McDonnell Douglas President's Award. She also earned the McDonnell Douglas Leadership award in 1996. She is a member of the Society of Flight Test

Nelda Lee enjoys the challenge of flying helicopters.

Engineers and is on the board of directors of Women in Aviation, International.

Nelda Lee has advice for young women thinking of careers in aviation. "Never stop learning. Education is so important. Learn as much as you can, then apply yourself. The competition is tough, so you need to be prepared. You will probably need at least a Master's degree. You will also need to focus on people. Learn to sell yourself when dealing with others. And, helping others along the way is an excellent way to accomplish that goal."[6]

Colonel Eileen
Marie Collins
(1956–)

On July 23, 1999, Air Force Colonel Eileen Collins was in command of the $2 billion Space Shuttle *Columbia.* There is only one commander on a shuttle. The commander is in charge of the shuttle and the crew and is responsible for the mission's success and safety. NASA (National Aeronautics and Space Administration) has been putting people into space for nearly forty years. "I've admired pilot astronauts and I've admired explorers of all kinds. Moreover, it was only a dream of mine that I would someday be one of them. It is my hope that all children, boys and girls, will see this mission and be inspired to reach for their dreams, because dreams do come true!" she said.

The shuttle would be flying 176 miles above the earth. Collins's job was to supervise the release of a

Eileen Collins

$1.5 billion telescope. The telescope is the most powerful telescope ever built. It allows scientists to see deeper into the universe. This was the first time a woman was in charge of the space shuttle.

In 1978, the first group of six female astronauts joined the astronaut corps. At the time of her flight, Collins was one of only twenty-seven American women who had flown into space.

"She is a person who has earned the title of commander, it has not been given to her," said Jeff Ashby, a Navy captain who flew as the other pilot crew member on the shuttle. "She started from very humble beginnings and worked her way up, and for that, I respect her tremendously. I think that respect is what's important and not either one of our genders."[1]

The mission was successful. After landing, Eileen said, "I have worked my whole life to get up here in space."

Vice President Al Gore greeted Eileen Collins when she returned to Houston, Texas. "She has not only equaled, but surpassed Amelia Earhart in the history of flight," he said.[2]

Eileen Collins was born on November 19, 1956, the second of four children. When Collins was nine, her parents separated, and money became scarce. "My dad was changing jobs, and my mom was trying to get a job, so we survived on food stamps for about six months," recalls Collins. It is a story she likes to tell student groups, hoping to inspire youngsters to follow their dreams. "Everybody has their own challenge," she says.

Eileen's parents, Jim and Rose Collins, describe her as a very ordinary person and a down-to-earth individual. She is very thoughtful. Nobody has handed her anything. Everything she is today, she has earned.

Eileen always wanted to be a pilot. When she was a child, her parents often took her to the airport to watch the airplanes.

"I always admired the astronauts, and I was very, very interested in the space program," Collins said. "As I got older I noticed, 'Hey, there's only men doing this job. What's going on?'"[3]

Collins's passion for flying took hold when she was just seven years old. In summer, she went to a local camp near Harris Hill, where, from the swimming pool, she had a good view of the gliders that were towed into the sky.

An average student in high school, she went on to study math and science at a local community college. While attending Corning Community College in Corning, New York, Collins flew for the first time on a commercial airline. "I looked out the window, down at the clouds and ocean of blue below me and thought, Wow! This is awesome! This is what I want to do." Collins knew her parents would never be able to afford lessons. "I didn't bother asking them for the money. I started saving it on my own." On her first solo flight, at age twenty, "the door [of the plane] popped open," she recalls. "But I said to myself, 'I'm just going to keep going.'"[4]

"I think the peer pressure on young women is a factor that keeps them from flying," Collins said. "When I first started taking flying lessons, people thought I was crazy. They would say, 'What? Nobody does that.' My friends from high school and college thought I was going off the deep end."[5]

"In high school," she said, "I began reading everything I could about famous pilots. I read about Amelia Earhart and the Women Airforce Service Pilots (WASP)." The WASP played an important role in World War II. They flew new airplanes from the factory to air bases. "Their stories inspired me. I admired the courage of these women to go and fly into dangerous situations!"

Eileen enjoyed math and science although she did not receive a lot of encouragement. Her father had been a surveyor, and she used to enjoy watching him spread his sketches across the kitchen table. She was drawn to the way he drew lines and angles and curves. The numbers he scrawled and the equations he carefully balanced were exquisite puzzles, and she wanted to solve them.[6]

Eileen had no idea what she wanted to do with her life when she graduated from high school. "I took bookkeeping, driver's ed, criminal law—stuff that I thought was interesting. I wanted to explore different areas I had not been exposed to. My attitude was, that if you do not try it how do you

know if you will like it. I did not really know what
I wanted to do," she remembers.[7] Eileen's parents felt
she was studying things she would need later in life.
When she was in high school, she never thought she
would be an astronaut. There were no women
astronauts then.

Everything changed for Eileen on graduation day.
As she crossed the stage to accept her diploma, she
began to ask herself, "What do I want to do? Forget
about peer pressure—where do your talents lie, and
what do you want to contribute to this world?"

Eileen enrolled at Corning Community College
in 1974. She doubled up on her math courses and
got a job to pay her tuition.

She received an associate's degree in mathematics/
science in 1976. She then transferred to Syracuse
University. There she majored in mathematics.
While at Syracuse University, she joined the Reserve
Officer Training Corps (ROTC).

By 1977, Eileen had saved $1,000 while working
nights at a pizza parlor. She could now take flying
lessons, and earn her pilot's license. She was nineteen
years old. It was the same year NASA began picking
women for the space shuttle program.

"That's when the career of being an astronaut
first became a reality to me. I really started looking
into doing this someday."

Eileen had good grades and flying experience.
She also had a letter of recommendation from her
ROTC supervisor. She became one of the first

women to go straight from college into Air Force pilot training. "That was by far the biggest break of my life, getting into pilot training." This is the point where Eileen set a goal. She was going to become an astronaut.

Eileen graduated from flight training in 1979. But despite her training and degree, Collins found some barriers ahead of her. When she earned her wings, Collins could not be assigned to fly most of the Air Force's airplanes. Women pilots, at that time, were not assigned to fighter aircraft because they were not allowed to fly combat missions.

Collins was not discouraged by those limitations. She became an instructor pilot, and flew the large C-141 cargo jets used to transport troops and equipment. She also spent two years as a C-141 aircraft commander. In 1983, Collins flew troops in the C-141 during the invasion of Grenada.

In 1986, Collins became an assistant professor of mathematics at the Air Force Academy. She was also an instructor pilot there.

Collins did not quit learning. She earned a degree in operations research from Stanford University. Then she earned another degree from Webster University.

By 1990, Eileen attended the Air Force's Test Pilot School. She was the second woman picked for that special school. During this period, she was picked for the astronaut program. In July 1991, Collins qualified as an astronaut and space shuttle pilot.

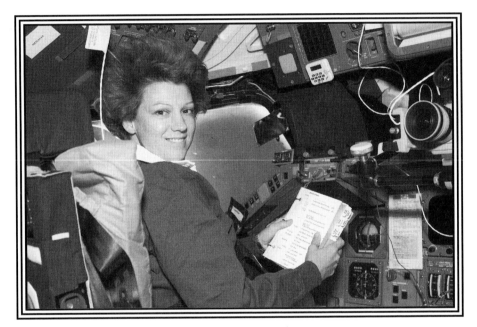

Eileen Collins, weightless in space.

In February 1995, Collins flew her first mission as a shuttle pilot. She flew the space shuttle to dock with the Russian Mir space station. During her first mission, she flew 129 orbits. She traveled over 2.9 million miles in 198 hours, 29 minutes.

Collins is also resourceful. After spending almost two hundred hours weightless in space, her hair was standing up. Collins used her technical skill and limited resources to figure out a solution for her hair. She made an exhaust-heat blower into a hair dryer. "I've never gotten my hair to look so good on Earth," she said.[8]

Collins is also a wife and the mother of a young daughter, Bridget Marie. She met her husband, Pat Youngs, when they were flying C-141s together in the Air Force.

Collins has flown three missions and logged more than five hundred hours in space. Today she has flown more than five thousand hours in more than thirty types of aircraft.

When not training for a shuttle mission, Collins enjoys running, golf, and camping. Often, she visits schools to inspire kids who may be searching for self-assurance or who haven't yet considered their options. She ends her talks by saying, "You can be an astronaut, but you need to do well in math and science, stay active in school, stay healthy—don't use drugs or use alcohol—exercise and eat right." She knows she is reaching some of the kids. "With the older kids you can see the wheels spinning. I know they are thinking, 'Hey, girls can be astronauts too.'"[9]

"Explore different areas to find where your talents lie," says Collins. "Do not be afraid to take a course because you may not get an A. Getting straight A's is not as important as what you learn."

Collins says, "It doesn't matter where you start, as long as you know where you're going."[10]

Martha King
(1945–)

When Martha King was a young girl, she never dreamed of being a pilot. When she was learning to fly in 1969, she had no idea where her wings would take her. Today, she has earned every pilot license category and class. She also has earned every flight and ground instructor rating offered by the Federal Aviation Administration (FAA). She is the only woman to accomplish this. Fewer than a dozen men have achieved this record. Her husband, John, is one of them.

Martha King was born Martha Rockwood on October 24, 1945, in Big Spring, Texas. Her father, Ralph, was an Air Force pilot and general. Her mother, Modest Hensley, was a former elementary school teacher.

Martha King

Martha remembers her first airplane ride. Her father had been transferred to the Philippines and she went with him. She recalls skipping up and down the aisles of a big four-engine propeller plane on the long hop from Hawaii to the Philippines.

The Air Force moved the Rockwoods all around the world. Martha, her older sister, Susy, and her parents lived in Guam and the Philippines. She also lived on various Air Force bases in the United States. After graduating from Fairborn High School, near Dayton, Ohio, Martha went to Indiana University. She enjoyed English and literature so she majored in comparative literature.

Her sister, Susy, also attended Indiana University. Susy had met a man named John King at a fraternity party. The two dated a few times, but they decided to be just friends. Susy suggested to John that he date her sister, Martha. John began to date Martha, and that began a relationship lasting more than thirty-eight years.

Martha and John married after her sophomore year. Martha was nineteen and John was twenty-one. After they graduated in 1966, they decided to go into business together. They had a unique idea. They welded a large fuel tank on the back of a truck. At night, they gassed up post office trucks, police cars, and other vehicles. This saved time in the morning. The drivers did not have to fill their own gas tanks. It was during this time that Martha learned to fly.

"I have always associated airplanes with faraway, exotic places and wonderful things," Martha remembers. However, to her, flying had not yet become a passion. It was not until she flew a fifty-five-mile flight alone that she knew what she wanted to do with her life. On this flight, her passion for flying suddenly rose to the surface. Since that flight, flying has been her life.

It was late one afternoon when Martha left Eagle Creek Airport in Indianapolis, Indiana, on her way to Richmond, Indiana. Rain showers at Richmond delayed her return to Indianapolis. After she took off, the lingering showers caused her to make some major flight detours on the way back to Eagle Creek Airport. "It began to get dark," she said, "and I had no training to fly at night." She told herself, "I can do this. I'm an intelligent person." She was determined. John and her flight instructor waited at the airport. They were nervous and worried that she might not make it. They also worried that if she did land safely she would never want to fly again.

Flying into the sunset, Martha King was enjoying herself. The lights twinkled below her like sparkling diamonds spread over a dark cloth. She turned on the airplane's lights and began looking for the airport. A road across the north end of Indianapolis made an unmistakable landmark. Martha swooped out of the sky making one of the smoothest landings she had ever experienced.

Martha stepped down from the airplane and said, "That was beautiful!" From that moment, she has been a passionate lover of aviation. "There is a different way you relate with life when you get above it," King said. "You get a whole new perspective on what's gone wrong and what's right."

Meanwhile, the Kings' business grew. Soon they were refueling over two thousand vehicles a night. They wanted to expand and sell franchises so they moved to California. Then, in 1974, the oil shortage forced them into bankruptcy. They had lost all their money.

Martha and her husband both took jobs with a company that taught aviation ground school around the country. They traveled from city to city, teaching student pilots the basic rules of safe flying.

After Martha and her husband had gained experience teaching ground school to student pilots, they decided to open their own business. At first, they taught live ground school classes. They later began putting the ground school on videotape and then on computer CDs. Today, King Schools and this pilot training program are responsible for training about half of all private pilots in the United States.

Martha has taught many interesting people to fly. Olympic gold medal winner Bruce Jenner was one of her students. Clint Eastwood wanted training as a helicopter pilot. He was going to Africa and wanted to be prepared for location shots in Africa.

Martha King has not taken a commercial airline flight in years. Most of her flying is done in the company's Cessna Citationjet. She uses it to fly to conventions, air shows, and other business appointments. Martha and John alternate between captain and copilot on each leg of a flight. At home in San Diego, she zips around in a small helicopter.

Martha King's favorite aircraft to fly is the blimp, a lighter-than-air aircraft.

Along with her husband, she is a back-up pilot for the Fujifilm airship. She has flown the blimp for major events like the Kentucky Derby and the Super Bowl.

"You are in constant pursuit of perfection with the blimp," she said. "You're flying something the size of a 747 as if it were a helicopter. You fly it off grass at an airport, but not from a runway. Every landing approach is different," she said. "A blimp must land exactly into the wind. Since its controls are mechanical rather than hydraulic, it is physically grueling, but lots of fun. Blimp flying is very challenging."

Martha King has a busy schedule, but she makes time for fun and to help others. Recently, she appeared on Microsoft's Flight Simulator 2000. King also volunteers with the FAA's National Aviation Safety Program. She helps produce video safety programs. In November 2000, President Clinton appointed Martha King to the First Flight Centennial Federal Advisory Board. This board will

Martha King has obtained every license a pilot can earn.

promote the 100th anniversary of flight, which occurs on December 17, 2003.

Martha King does not like to talk about her accomplishments or her personal rewards. She prefers to be a means for others to achieve their goals and improve themselves in flying and in life. "I hope I can leave people better off and happier than when I met them," she says.

Martha King would like to see more women in aviation. "Aviation provides great role models," she says. "It also provides satisfying and good paying careers . . . and," she adds, "we definitely need more women flight instructors."

Martha King is one of those role models she talks about. All her life she has been setting goals and writing them down. "Writing them down can make your goals become clear to you," Martha says. "Putting them on paper can also be scary. It takes courage to put them on paper because you are making a commitment. It makes what may seem like an unattainable goal suddenly very real."

One goal Martha set was to pilot a jet airplane. "It took me about ten years to achieve this goal," she said. "I kept my eyes open for every opportunity, and continuously improved my flying skills."

Martha's achievements prove that a woman with goals and focus can be successful. "I believe people can do anything they want to do if they face their fear and walk through it. I was a shy girl growing up. To be successful I had to become an outgoing person and interact with other people. I had to learn to get up on a stage and do public speaking. I learned that if I was to be successful I'd have to just get out there and do it." Martha was also motivated. "If I could get out there and do public speaking, I could get the things in life I wanted."

"There are still more issues women have to overcome," she says. "There is one of economics. Flight training is expensive. Women do not generally make as much as men. Sometimes a woman's family or children are not comfortable with the risk of flying."

"Have a passion for what you are doing!" Martha says. She believes that the journey through life is more important than the destination. "There is no point dragging yourself through life, and not enjoying it on a daily basis. If you do what you love to do you will be good at it, and you will be successful."

Chapter Notes

Preface

1. Samuel S. Whitt, "Miss Harriet Quimby," *National Aeronautics*, Spring 1973, p. 23.

2. H.V. "Pat" Reilly, "From The Balloon to the Moon-a Chronology of New Jersey's Amazing Aviation History," H.V. Publishers, 1992, p. 5.

Chapter 1. Harriet Quimby (1875–1912)

1. Harriet Quimby, "An American Girl's Daring Exploits," *Leslie's Illustrated Weekly*, April 16, 1912, p. 568.

2. Manistee County, Michigan Census, dated June 18, 1880.

3. Harriet Quimby, "The Artist Colony at Monterey," *Sunday Call*, August 25, 1901, p. 10.

4. Elizabeth Anna Semple, "Harriet Quimby, America's First Woman Aviator," *Overland Monthly*, December 1911, p. 526.

5. "Women in Trousers, Daring Aviator," *The New York Times*, May 11, 1911, Vol. LX, no. 19, p. 6.

6. Ibid.

7. Semple, p. 531.

8. Ibid., p. 530.

9. Harriet Quimby, "An American Girl's Daring Exploits," *Good Housekeeping*, September 1912, p. 568.

10. Elizabeth Hiatt Gregory, "Women's Record in Aviation, September 12, 1912, *Good Housekeeping*, unpaged.

11. "Beauty and the Bleriot," *Aviation Quarterly*, Vol. 6, 1980, p. 69.

Chapter 2. Bessie Coleman (1892–1926)

1. Elois Coleman Patterson, *Memoirs of the Late Bessie Coleman Aviatrix: Pioneer of the Negro People in Aviation* (privately published by Elois Coleman Patterson, 1969), p. 12.

2. Doris L. Rich, *Queen Bess, Daredevil Aviator* (Washington, D.C.: Smithsonian Institution Press, 1993), p. 23.

3. PBS Online, "The American Experience: Fly Girls," n.d., <http//www.pbs.org/wgbh/amex/flygirls/peopleevents/pandeAMEX02.html> (December 17, 2001).

4. "Shuffle Along Company Gives Fair Flyer Cup," *Chicago Defender*, October 8, 1921, p. 2.

5. Doris Rich, "My Quest for Queen Bess," *Air & Space Smithsonian*, August/September 1994, p. 56.

6. Constance Porter Uzelac, "Bessie Coleman," American National Biography Online, February 2000, <http://www.anb.org/articles/20/20-01758.html.>.

7. Rich, p. 110.

Chapter 3. Amelia Earhart (1897–1937)

1. "Amelia Earhart," National Headquarters Civil Air Patrol, Maxwell Air Force Base, Alabama, 1992, p. 8.

2. Amelia Earhart, *The Fun of It*, (New York: Brewer, Warren & Putnam, 1932), p. 23.

3. Ibid., p. 25.

4. Ibid.

5. Ibid., p. 48.

6. "'Two Legends of Aviation': Amelia Earhart's Friendship Flight," World Book, Inc., p. 1, n.d., http://www2.worldbook.com/features/aviators/html/av12.htm>.

7. Earhart, p. 61.

8. C.V. Glines, "'Lady Lindy': The Remarkable Life of Amelia Earhart," p. 4, <http://www.thehistorynet.com/aviationhistory/articles/1997/0797_tex.html> (December 17, 2001).

9. Claudia M. Oakes, "United States Women in Aviation, 1930-1939," (Washington, D.C.: Smithsonian Institution Press, 1985), p. 25.

10. Wendy Boase, *The Sky's the Limit* (New York: MacMillian Publishing Company, Inc., 1979), p. 89.

11. Glines, p. 7.

12. Boase, p. 89.

Chapter 4. Anne Morrow Lindbergh (1906–2001)

1. Nathan A. Ferguson, "Anne Lindbergh Leaves Aviation, Literary Legacies," *AOPA Pilot*, April 2001, p. 52.

2. Joyce Milton, *Lost Eden* (New York: HarperCollins Publishers, 1993), p. 183.

3. Ferguson, p. 52.

4. Anne Morrow Lindbergh, *North to the Orien*t (New York: Harcourt, Brace, & World, Inc., 1935), pp. 137–138.

5. Lindbergh Foundation Web site, <http://www.lindberghfoundation.org/> (April 5, 2002).

6. Lindbergh, p. 137.

7. Anne Morrow Lindbergh, *A Gift from the Sea* (New York: Pantheon Books, Inc., 1955), p. 109.

Chapter 5. Jacqueline Cochran (1910?–1980)

1. Maryann Bucknum Brinley, *Jackie Cochran: The Autobiography of the Greatest Woman Pilot in Aviation History* (New York: Bantam Books, 1987), p. 49.

2. "American National Biography Online," Online Product Department, Oxford University Press, <http://www.anbiorg/articles/bin/advanced-search.html> (April 6, 2002).

3. Brinley, p. 49.

4. "The American Experience: Fly Girls" Thirteen WNET New York, p.1, n.d., <http://www.pbs.org/wgbh/amex/flygirls/peopleevents/pandeAMEX01.html> (December 17, 2001).

5. Ibid.

6. Gene Burnett, "A Florida Native Born To Fly," *Florida Living*, September 1977, p. 88.

7. The American Experience: Fly Girls, p. 1.

8. Brinley, p. 100.

9. Ibid., p. 18.

10. Burnett, p. 88.

Chapter 6. Betty Skelton Frankman (1926–)

1. Author interview with Betty Skelton Frankman, April 23, 2001.

2. Ibid.

3. Ibid.

4. Betty Skelton, *Little Stinker* (Winter Haven, Fla., Cross Press, 1977), pp. 18–19.

5. Ibid., p. 19.

6. Ibid.

7. Skelton, p. 89.

8. Author interview with Betty Skelton Frankman, April 23, 2001.

9. Skelton, p. 23.

10. Author interview with Betty Skelton Frankman, April 23, 2001.

11. Anne Cooper, "Betty Skelton: An Exceptional Woman," *Pilot Magazine*, September/October 1998, p. 18.

12. Cooper, p. 19.

13. Ibid.

14. Author interview with Betty Skelton Frankman, April 23, 2001.

Chapter 7. Bonnie Tiburzi (1948–)

1. Bonnie Tiburzi, *Takeoff! The Story of America's First Woman Pilot for a Major Airline* (New York: Crown Publishers, 1984), p. 9.

2. Ibid.

3. Ibid., p. 11.

4. Ibid., p. 12.

5. Author interview with Bonnie Tiburzi, March 14, 2001.

6. Ibid.

7. Ibid.

8. Tiburzi, p. 65.

9. Ibid., p. 69.

10. Ibid., p. 71.

11. Tiburzi, p. 34.

12. Ibid., p. 85.

13. Author interview with Bonnie Tiburzi, December 27, 2001.

14. Author interview with Bonnie Tiburzi, December 27, 2001.

15. Ibid.

16. Tiburzi, p. 143.

17. Ibid.

18. Ibid., p. 144.

19. Ibid.

20. Author interview with Bonnie Tiburzi, December 27, 2001.

21. Ibid.

22. Ibid.

Chapter 8. Nelda K. Lee (1946–)

1. Author interview with Nelda Lee, March 14, 2001.

2. Ibid.

3. Ibid.

4. Whirly-Girls: International Women Helicopter Pilots Roster, Menlo Park, Calif., 1994, p. 32.

5. Author interview with Nelda Lee, March 14, 2001.

6. Ibid.

Chapter 9. Colonel Eileen Marie Collins (1956–)

1. Robin Suriano, "From a Small Town to the Stars: The Story of Eileen Collins," *Florida Today*, July 19, 1999, <http://www.flatoday.com/space/explore/stories/1999b/071999c.htm>.

2. Marcia Gilelman, "Commander in Space," *Woman Pilot*, September/October 1999, p. 19.

3. Suriano.

4. Jane Sims Podesta, Anne-Marie O'Neill, and Laurel Calkins, *People Weekly*, May 11, 1998, p. 225.

5. Suriano.

6. Amy Laboda, "Col. Eileen Collins: An Ordinary Girl with Extraordinary Dreams," *Aviation for Women*, September/October 1999, p. 24.

7. Ibid., p. 26.

8. Podesta, p. 225.

9. Laboda, p. 28.

10. Suriano.

Chapter 10. Martha King (1945–)

1. All quotations in Chapter 10 were cited from the author's interview with Martha King, June 22, 2001.

Further Reading

Books

Briggs, Carole S. *At the Controls: Women in Aviation*. Minneapolis, Minn.: Lerner Publications Company, 1991.

Hart, Philip. *Up in the Air: The Story of Bessie Coleman*. Minneapolis, Minn.: Carolrhoda Books, 1996.

Howe, Jane Moore. *Amelia Earhart: Young Air Pioneer*. Carmel, Ind.: Patria Press, Inc., 1999.

Leder, Jane. *Amelia Earhart*. Great Mysteries - Opposing Viewpoints. San Diego, Calif.: Greenhaven Press, 1989.

Lindbergh, Reeve. *Nobody Owns the Sky: The Story of "Brave Bessie" Coleman*. Cambridge, Mass.: Candlewick Press, 1998.

McGuire, Nina and Sammons, Sandra Wallus. *Jacqueline Cochran; America's Fearless Aviator*. Lake Buena Vista, Fla.: Tailored Tours Publications, 1997.

McLoone, Margo. *Women Explorers of the Air*. Mankato, Minn.: Capstone Books, 2000.

Pasternak, Ceel and Thornburg, Linda. *Cool Careers for Girls in Air and Space*. Atascadero, Calif.: Impact Publications, 2001.

Skelton, Betty. *Little Stinker*, Winter Haven, Fla.: Cross Press, 1977.

Video

Fly Girls, PBS Home Video, WGBH Educational Foundation, 2000.

Internet Addresses

Women in Aviation Resource Center
<www.women-in-aviation.com>

The Ninety-Nines – International Organization of Women Pilots Association
<http://www.ninety-nines.org/>

Women of NASA
<www.quest.arc.nasa.gov/women/intro.html>

Women in Aviation International

Index